CLASSICAL MUSIC COLORING BOOK

---

8 Opera Composers
From Verdi to Strauss

ARTHUR BENJAMIN

This page intentionally left blank.

ABOUT THE BOOK

If you are a classical music fan or want to raise your child as such, this coloring book is a must. Color 8 titans of opera music including Verdi, Puccini, Rossini, Mozart and many more. All pictures are arranged with beautiful backgrounds reflecting each composer's individual life and work.

CONTENTS

This page intentionally left blank.

LA TRAVIATA

Giuseppe Verdi

Plate 1.

TOSCA

Giacomo Puccini

Plate 2.

The Barber of
Seville

Gioachino Rossini

Plate 3.

Wolfgang Mozart

Plate 4.

Parsifal

Richard Wagner

Plate 5.

Gaetano Donizetti

Plate 6.

Richard Strauss

Plate 7.

George Frideric Handel

Plate 8.

ABOUT THE BOOK

If you are a classical music fan or want to raise your child as such, this coloring book is a must. Color 8 titans of opera music including Verdi, Puccini, Rossini, Mozart and many more. All pictures are arranged with beautiful backgrounds reflecting each composer's individual life and work.

This page intentionally left blank.

www.ingramcontent.com/pod-product-compliance
Lightning Source LLC
Chambersburg PA
CBHW081236020426
42331CB00012B/3204